Henry the Owl

Story by Wendy Kanno ◆ Illustrations by Bob Reese

Dominie Press, Inc.

Henry is a crying owl.

Henry has a crying towel.

Henry Owl does not cry,

"WHO!"

Henry Owl cries,

"BOO WHO WHO."

He sleeps all day.

He cries all night.

Henry gives animals

such a fright.

13

such a fright.

Henry is a crying owl.

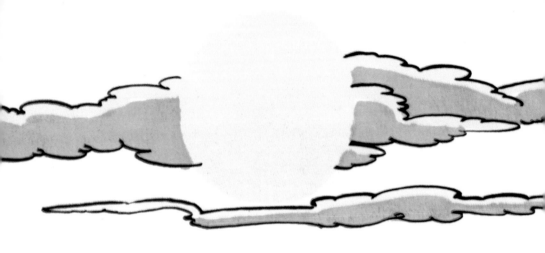

Henry has a crying towel.

Henry Owl
does not cry,

"WHO!"

18

Henry Owl cries,

"BOO
WHO
WHO."

I am a
Twenty-Word Book

My twenty words are:

a	has
all	He
animals	Henry
Boo	is
cry	night
(cries)	not
(crying)	owl
day	sleeps
does	such
fright	towel
gives	Who

Published by:

🐚 **Dominie Press, Inc.**

1949 Kellogg Avenue
Carlsbad, California 92008 USA

www.dominie.com
ISBN 0-7685-2221-8
Printed in Singapore by PH Productions Pte Ltd
1 2 3 4 5 PH 07 06 05